A People in Focus Book

STANDING UP FOR AMERICA

A BIOGRAPHY OF LEE IACOCCA

Patricia Haddock

₽ DILLON PRESS, INC.
Minneapolis, Minnesota 55415

Library of Congress Cataloging-in-Publication Data

Haddock, Patricia.
  Standing up for America.

  (People in focus)
  Bibliography: p.
  Includes index.
  Summary: A biography of the businessman who saved the Chrysler
Corporation from bankruptcy.
    1. Iacocca, Lee A.—Juvenile literature.   2. Automobile industry
and trade—United States—Biography—Juvenile literature.   3. Business-
men—United States—Biography—Juvenile literature.   [1. Iacocca, Lee
A.   2. Businessmen.   3. Automobile industry and trade]
I. Title.   II. Series.
HD9710.U52I246   1987   338.7'6292'0924[B] [92]   86-32965
ISBN 0-87518-362-X

Dillon Press, Inc., 242 Portland Avenue South
Minneapolis, Minnesota 55415

Printed in the United States of America
1 2 3 4 5 6 7 8 9 10 95 94 93 92 91 90 89 88 87

Contents

Photographic Acknowledgements

The photographs are reproduced through the courtesy of Dr. David L. Lewis of the University of Michigan School of Business Administration, the Chrysler Corporation, and UPI/Bettmann Archive.

Introduction

One of America's most admired people

On the afternoon of July 13, 1978, Lee Iacocca left his boss's office, shocked by what had just happened.

That morning, Iacocca was president of Ford Motor Company. He worked in a beautifully decorated, private office at the Glass House—Ford World Headquarters. When he traveled, he flew in a private, company jet. He was driven to and from home in a chauffered limousine. The morning of July 13, 1978, Iacocca was one of the most powerful men in the United States.

The afternoon of July 13, 1978, Lee Iacocca had lost his job.

Iacocca remembers that day more than any other in his years in the car business. He was angry and hurt. But instead of causing him to retire from the auto industry, the firing made him determined to try again and to succeed. Lee Iacocca had to show his ex-boss and the world that he was not going to walk away from the work he loved.

Iacocca took on the back-breaking job of saving the Chrysler Corporation from bankruptcy. If Chrysler went bankrupt, it would go out of business. More than 100,000 employees in seven states would lose their jobs. The bankruptcy would affect another 400,000 people who worked for Chrysler suppliers and dealers. The Chrysler job was a challenge that many men and women wouldn't think of taking on. But Lee Iacocca thrives on challenges, and saving Chrysler was the biggest challenge of his career.

It took Iacocca three years to turn the failing company around. He drew on all his experience and abilities, and there were times during the struggle to save Chrysler that he thought he was losing his mind.

Iacocca had to "beg" Congress and the banks to trust him with more than a billion dollars. Then he had to find a way to pay the money back.

He led his employees and fellow executives on the path of sacrifice to save the company. People in all parts of the company took salary and benefit cuts, and many were laid off or fired.

He convinced the American public to buy Chrysler cars because they were quality cars made by a quality company. "If you can find a better car, buy it," Lee Iacocca told us in his television commercials, and he meant it.

Financial World, a business magazine, called Iacocca "the glue that held the Chrysler Corporation together when the company was about to fall apart."

Lee Iacocca did what he set out to do. Exactly five years after Iacocca was fired from Ford, he announced that Chrysler would soon repay the huge sum it had borrowed. The company was making a profit every quarter, and the future looked bright.

"This is the day that makes the. . .miserable years all seem worthwhile," Iacocca said in his speech to announce the loan payback. "We at Chrysler borrow money the old-fashioned way. We pay it back."

Saving Chrysler crowned his automobile career, but it is just one of the things Iacocca can be proud of:

- He was the creative force behind the automobile some people think is one of the greatest cars ever made—the Ford Mustang.
- He was a major force behind the efforts to restore the Statue of Liberty and Ellis Island.
- He had a long and successful marriage and raised two fine daughters.
- He is a celebrity, a best-selling author, and one of America's most admired people.

Perhaps only in America could the son of poor Italian immigrants have the chance to succeed as he has done. But his successes were not without failures and mistakes.

Throughout his life, Lee Iacocca has known failure and suffered the pain of personal loss. When he has been tempted to give up, to take the easy way, Iacocca has always found the energy and the courage to keep going because he doesn't believe in giving up. This is his story.

Chapter/One

When you aim at anything, you are sure to hit it

Much of Lee's strength, courage, and persistence came from his father, Nick Iacocca. Nick believed life has its ups and downs, everyone has a share of bad times, and each person has to find a way of dealing with these bad times. This was a belief that would run throughout the life of Lee Iacocca.

Lee's dad, Nicola Iacocca, was born and raised in the small Italian town of San Marco near Naples. It was a poor town where many people lived underground in caves. In the late 1890s and early 1900s, most strong young boys in that area ended up as farm laborers. This was not a job Nicola's family wanted for him. Since his other choice—a life among the dangers of Rome—was just as bad, Nicola decided to come to the United States. He would work a while, save some money, and, as soon as he could afford it, he would bring his mother over from Italy to live with him.

Nicola left his family and village and bought a ticket on a ship bound for the United States. This was a dangerous journey for a twelve-year-old boy. Yet many young boys in those days did just what Nicola Iacocca did. They left family and friends to travel across the Atlantic Ocean. They were searching for jobs and were desperate for a chance to make something of their lives in a land where they didn't even know the language.

From 1892 to 1924, immigrants from Europe entered the United States at Ellis Island. Nicola arrived there in 1902—just one small, frightened boy among thousands of other poor people determined to make something of themselves in America.

Lee says his father believed America was a land where you could become anything you wanted to become. All you had to do, his dad told him, was work hard enough to get it.

Work in the early 1900s meant fourteen-hour days of hard labor. Most workers had no paid vacations, holidays, or sick time. Even though Nicola was only twelve, he wasted no time. He went to Allentown, Pennsylvania, and went to work at a restaurant his uncle owned. Allentown was a good place for the young boy so far from home. Its hills reminded him of Italy, and he loved the town's clean streets with their neat homes.

According to Richard Gambino, a writer and teacher, "to Italian immigrants . . . work is . . . a matter of pride." Like other Italian newcomers in America, Nicola worked hard. He scrimped and saved and after a while he opened his own hot dog restaurant. He also bought the first of many Ford cars he would own over the years—a Model T.

Even though Nicola worked hard, he also took time to learn about his new country by listening to stories of America's fight for freedom from the British. Since he wanted to be a true American, he began calling himself "Nick"—a more American name. He studied citizenship, took the tests to become an American citizen, and passed. Nick Iacocca was now truly an American.

In April 1921, Nick finally returned to Italy to bring his mother to the United States to live with him. While in Italy, he met and fell in love with Antoinette Perrotto, a shoemaker's daughter. His two-week visit stretched into three months as he courted the sixteen-year-old girl.

Courtship in Italy in those days was not quick and easy. Nick visited Antoinette's family over and over again until they knew him well enough for him to ask for their daughter's hand in marriage. The young Antoinette and her parents agreed, and the couple was married in a church in San Marco. Nick headed back to the United States with both his mother and a brand new wife. But the Iacocca family was almost destroyed before it had a chance to grow and prosper.

On the ocean crossing, Antoinette came down with typhoid fever. Immigration officers at Ellis Island should have kept Antoinette from entering the United States. No one who had a "loathsome or dangerous contagious disease could enter the United States." And typhoid fever was one of these diseases.

Nick Iacocca, though, was not going to be stopped. He convinced the immigration officers that his bride was only seasick. Surprisingly, they believed him, and Nick brought both his mother and his bride home to Allentown. The Iacoccas were on their way to becoming a family.

Nick opened a new restaurant called the Orpheum Wiener House and invested in U-Drive-It, a car rental business. Most of the more than thirty cars Nick rented were his personal favorites, Fords. Nick's love of Fords lasted all his life.

Lee was born on October 15, 1924, two years after his sister Delma. He was christened Lido Anthony. His father's businesses and real estate investments were booming. Nick was building a small fortune, but in 1929 the Iacoccas lost almost everything Nick had made.

During the Great Depression, American businesses and investors lost huge amounts of money, banks closed, and many Americans could not get their savings out of their accounts. People lost their businesses, jobs, and homes. Nick Iacocca lost much of his property, his businesses closed, and the Iacoccas almost lost their home.

Nick refused to give up. The Iacoccas had a deep belief in God and the power of prayer. Lee believes that that faith and Nick's courage and determination helped them through the bad times.

Nick also knew that people have to eat. When times were bad, he believed, the food business would still be needed. Nick opened a new restaurant and began to rebuild the family fortune. After a while, he invested in two movie theaters. To attract more people to his theaters, Nick held "promotions"—ways of getting people to come to the movies or to buy something. One time Nick gave free tickets to the ten kids with the dirtiest faces.

Nick liked all kinds of automobiles and was the first person in Allentown to own a motorcycle, an old Harley Davidson. Nick, however, had a hard time riding the bike. In fact, he was tossed off it so often that he finally sold it. By then he had come to hate bikes of all kinds and refused to allow Lee to own one. If Lee wanted to ride a bike, he had to borrow a friend's, but he learned how to drive a car as soon as he was old enough. Later in his life, Lee joked that he was the only boy in Allentown to go straight from a tricycle to a car.

The Iacocca family was close—so close that Lee says it felt like one person with four parts. Lee's parents always made time for him and Delma. On Sundays, which were saved for the family, a stream of relatives and friends filled the Iacocca house. His mother often cooked their favorite pasta dishes and, according to Lee, the world's best pizza.

Lee had a deep and special relationship with his father. Lee liked to do things that pleased his dad, such as getting good grades. Whenever Lee won an award at school, he made sure his dad was one of the first people to know.

Nick always told Lee that he could come to him with anything—good news, bad news, or trouble—and Nick would stand behind him. Lee says that he and Nick often hugged and kissed each other. "People getting along is based on people respecting one another: talking openly and asking openly what your kids need, or what the parents need from the kid," Lee said in a recent interview. "But transcending [going beyond] all of that, more than anything else, is deeply caring for one another."

Life outside the Iacocca home presented tough problems for the son of Italian immigrants. When Lee was a boy, prejudice against immigrant families—Italian, Jewish, Irish, Polish, Chinese—was common. Other Americans called them names and thought they were inferior.

Lee took a lot of teasing for being Italian. For a long time, he thought "Dago" and "Wop" were places on the map rather than insulting names for Italians. Teachers even called him "a little wop" under their breath.

When Lee was in sixth grade, he found out what prejudice really meant. He ran for student office and lost the election by a vote of twenty-two to twenty. Lee felt bitterly disappointed, but he did not discover what had really happened until the next day. A fellow student called him a "dumb wop" and explained that there were only thirty-eight students in the class, but forty-two votes had been cast. The election had been rigged so that Lee was sure to lose.

The injustice didn't stop there. When Lee complained to his teacher that fake votes had been cast, she refused to do anything. The incident affected Lee so deeply that he grew up to hate prejudice of any kind.

Despite such problems, Lee enjoyed school. He was a shy child who studied hard. His English and Latin teacher says that he knew what he had to do and did it. No one had to force Lee to study. He earned spending money after school and on weekends by carting shoppers' groceries home in his wagon. As a teenager, he worked at a fruit market on weekends. In between, Lee studied. He had to do his school work before he did anything else, and he could play only when he was finished studying.

In high school Lee began to outgrow his shyness. He began playing football, baseball, and even thought of a baseball career. He swam and ice skated. In the ninth grade he won the school presidency, but the victory made him cocky and "big-headed." Because he forgot the needs of the voters, his fellow students, he lost the election in the second semester.

Lee believes that one of the most valuable groups he joined in high school was the debating team. In a debate, people take sides on an issue or problem. They argue with each other. Sometimes, one person takes both sides of the subject and argues with him or herself.

Debating taught Lee to think on his feet and to express his ideas. Today, even with that experience behind him, Lee says he still gets nervous before he speaks to groups of people.

In his sophomore year Lee almost died from a terrible disease, called rheumatic fever, that kept him in bed for six months. During that time, he suffered constant, intense pain. Every joint—knees, ankles, elbows, and wrists—hurt and hurt terribly. Rheumatic fever could kill and kill painfully.

Despite the pain, Lee refused to lie in bed and do nothing. He read all kinds of books. His sister Delma carried assignments and homework to and from Lee and his teachers. He kept up his studies, and even made the school's honor roll that semester.

Lee Iacocca's struggle against the effects of rheumatic fever was typical of how Lee dealt with problems later in life. He came from a family that refused to accept defeat, no matter what happened.

Lee spent six months in bed while the disease ran its deadly course. When he finally returned to school, he was forty pounds lighter and he could no longer think of a baseball career. In fact, he could not actively play in any sport. Lee swallowed his disappointment and looked for other things he could do. He studied more than ever before and began to play chess, bridge, and poker. Since he couldn't be active in sports, he became the swim team manager.

Lee graduated from high school with a long list of honors—class honor roll, National Honor Society, senior class presidency, membership in the Latin Club and debating society. He is quoted in his yearbook as writing "When you aim at anything, you are sure to hit it." Lee Iacocca was becoming a master at the art of hitting what he aimed at.

When Japan bombed Pearl Harbor, and the United States entered World War II, Lee was unable to serve in the military. The rheumatic fever left scars that kept him from enlisting. Since he could not defend his country, he buried himself in his schoolwork. At Lehigh College he studied engineering and psychology because he wanted to learn how both machines and people work. His class spent time working in a hospital ward for the mentally ill. That experience taught Lee how to judge people quickly from a first meeting.

Lee took classes six days a week to earn a college degree in as little time as possible. His classmates often teased him for studying so hard since most of them were willing to take a full four years to finish college. They thought five days of school with three months of summer vacation was just fine. Some students even cut their classes, but not Lee.

Lee's father, like many immigrant fathers, wanted his son to go to college and to take advantage of everything the parents could not have. This was one of the reasons people came to America—to give their children more than they could have had if they had stayed in their native lands.

Lee decided to finish his studies in three years instead of four. He could only do that by attending summer school each year. Lee accepted that kind of difficult class schedule because he believed that you had to concentrate and use your time to its fullest if you wanted to succeed. He completed college in eight straight semesters, including summer sessions.

In 1945, just before Lee graduated, a Ford Motor Company executive came to Lehigh College and offered Lee a job. Lee also had an offer of a fellowship to Princeton to study for his graduate degree. Since Ford agreed to wait for him while he did his graduate work, Lee went to Princeton. One year later, Lee arrived at Ford's River Rouge plant near Detroit, Michigan, to begin his career with Ford. He had his master's degree and was determined to go as far and as fast as he could at Ford.

The Ford training program began with a ten-day introduction to the company and continued for eighteen months. Each trainee worked in every part of the plant— from stoking the red-hot ovens to tightening screws on the assembly line to the test track and plant hospital.

Franklin Zimmerman, a fellow trainee and later a good friend of Lee Iacocca's, went through the program ahead of Lee. Zimmerman believes that the Ford training gave them a great chance to learn the auto business from the ground up. Lee, he says, was one of the best trainees to go through the program.

Lee convinced his managers that his training period should be shortened since he had come to Ford with an extra year's education. Ford managers agreed. But at the end of Lee's year-long training program, he decided that he didn't want to be an engineer. Lee didn't know then that his decision would make success at Ford much harder to achieve. The drive to succeed that had helped him come so far would soon be put to the test.

Chapter / Two

Mistakes are part of living

Lee Iacocca went through the Ford training program during a time of economic growth—the late 1940s. More and
more people began buying cars as men and women
returned from Europe after World War II. A car boom
spread across the United States, and dealers were hard
pressed to fill orders. Buyers waited months for their cars.
When they finally took delivery, their automobiles filled
the roads throughout the country. To handle all this new
traffic, freeways and toll roads started to appear. The automobile was becoming America's favorite machine and its
most convenient form of mass transportation.

Lee decided that he really liked working with people,
not machines. Sales, not engineering, was the place he
wanted to be at Ford. His managers at River Rouge
weren't happy with his decision since his training had
already cost the company time and money. They allowed
him to leave and even gave him a letter of recommenda-

tion, but they would not help him find a job in sales. Now Lee was on his own. He decided to go to New York.

Lee's friend, Frank Zimmerman, had also left the world of engineering and was working in truck sales in New York. Lee went to see him. First, like all young men in a big city, they visited all the tourist sites and the night spots. Then Lee got down to the business of finding a job.

Lee made an appointment to meet with the Ford district sales manager. He knew he had to make a good first impression since he had no sales experience and his background and education wouldn't help him get a job. Lee had to rely on the force of his speech and his personality.

When Lee arrived for his appointment, the district manager was out. Lee met the manager's two assistants. One of the assistants took Lee's letter of recommendation from the River Rouge plant, but he never even looked at it. Instead, he kept reading his newspaper. The other assistant looked Lee up and down and asked a few questions. Then he lost interest in Lee and let him leave.

Lee felt crushed. This was his chance to get into the one area of the auto business he wanted to be in. And yet, he couldn't even get a fair hearing from the men who had the power to hire him.

The tough Iacocca spirit wouldn't let him give up. Lee tried again and made another appointment. This time he was interviewed by the district manager, but that interview went no better than the first one with the man's two assistants. The manager told Iacocca that he would never succeed in sales.

For a while, Lee thought about giving up the idea of working for Ford. Then he remembered his dad's words, "Never give up," and he decided to give it one more chance.

This time Lee left New York and went to see Charles Beacham, the sales manager at Ford's office in Chester, Pennsylvania. Beacham saw in Lee a tremendous energy and drive to succeed. He gave the determined young man a job as a field manager. The position was considered the "lowest form of life in sales," but Lee took on his new duties with eagerness.

Part of Lee's job was to sell to car fleet purchasing agents who bought large "fleets" of cars for big companies. At first Lee found this work quite difficult. He was still shy and awkward, and the thought of picking up the phone made him nervous. He practiced what he was going to say over and over again before he made each call.

Lee's fears, though, didn't stop him. Within two months he was promoted to truck sales, and soon he began selling cars, too. Once, to get rid of a supply of used cars, Lee drove one around the countryside until he found someone who owned a very old car. Then he sold that person the newer used car he was driving. He did that over and over again. In three weeks he sold the entire lot of used cars.

Lee also went out on the road to hold week-long training classes at different places each week. This was the kind of work Lee loved. He believed that the dealers were the heart of the auto business, and his job gave him a chance to find out what they needed. He listened carefully to what they said, even if it wasn't very nice.

Lee believes that talking to the people in the offices he visited gave him self-confidence and sharpened his speaking skills. He worked hard and put in long hours to learn all he could about the car business. It helped to have one of the best teachers in the country.

Lee admired Charles Beacham a great deal. His boss was a lot like his dad—a tough yet fair teacher. Beacham, like Lee's dad, expected Lee to do his best, and then he would push Lee to do even better. Beacham taught Lee that mistakes are a part of living. He expected his people to admit their mistakes, and he respected people who honestly faced their faults and failings. All a person could do was try to correct mistakes and not make the same mistake more than once.

As Lee started to have some success in the auto business, his personal life began to improve, too. Romance entered Lee's life when he first saw Mary McCleary, a Ford receptionist at Chester. He met her a month later at a company party. A friend of Mary's rescued her from a man who was bothering her and introduced her to Lee. Mary thought Lee was skinny and very shy—and she was right—but she liked him, and they started dating.

Mary and Lee saw each other around Lee's busy schedule. On weeknights, he often worked. Since he went to his parent's house on the weekends, they could see each other only if Mary went with him to see his parents. Lee and Mary were rarely alone. When Lee finally proposed marriage, Mary wasn't sure they should get married. She turned him down, but while they continued to date on and off, the romance went through some tough times.

Lee's business life and personal life seemed to mirror each other because his professional life began to suffer, too. Bad luck struck the Ford Motor Company in the early 1950s. Sales were down, and Ford fired or laid off many employees all over the country. Lee was lucky. Instead of losing his job, he was offered a lower level position. He was tempted to leave but pushed the thought aside. Instead, he doubled his efforts to succeed. In six months he had his old job back, and in six more months he was promoted to a higher position as assistant sales manager for the district.

Lee kept working hard, and usually he was successful. But one time, in 1956, Lee had egg on his face—and everywhere else.

In 1956 Ford Motor Company executives decided to "promote" auto safety, and they decided to show off one of their new safety features—the padding on the dashboard. The company launched the safety promotion by distributing a film showing how effective the crash padding was. In the film, eggs dropped from a two-story building bounced off a well-padded car dash without breaking. That was the ultimate in safety.

Just showing the film to his salespeople wasn't good enough for Lee Iacocca. He decided that he would impress his staff more if he could prove to them how well the padding worked. He would drop his own eggs on his own strip of padding.

Lee called in 1,100 Ford salespeople and set up his demonstration on a stage in front of them. He climbed a ladder with a carton of fresh eggs and looked down at the strip of padding spread below him on the floor. This, he hoped, would be one demonstration that his staff would never forget.

Lee dropped egg number one. It missed the padding and splattered on the floor of the stage. The audience roared with laughter. Lee and his assistant moved the ladder.

Lee dropped egg number two just as his assistant moved. The egg bounced off his assistant's shoulder and broke.

Eggs number three and four hit the padding. Unlike the eggs in the film, though, these eggs broke.

Finally, egg number five hit the padding and came to rest, unbroken. The audience stood and applauded.

Lee learned a valuable lesson that day. Always rehearse what you want to say and do before you step in front of an audience.

Lee's egg-splattered safety demonstration was no more successful than the safety campaign was. Since sales were down across the nation, Lee set out to find the key to selling cars. After much thought and brainstorming— coming up with a great number of ideas—Lee decided that what the public wanted most was a monthly payment they could afford.

Here was his plan. A customer could buy a new 1956 Ford with a 20 percent downpayment. The monthly payments would be $56 a month for three years. Lee called it "56 for '56," and it was a brand new idea in those days. The idea of consumer credit—buying a product and paying for it over a long period of time—was new. Most people saved first, then paid cash for what they wanted.

To make sure the campaign worked, Lee and a friend put together a promotion. They made cards called "wudjatak," pronounced "would you take." When Ford salespeople saw a used car in good condition, they checked the car's value in a pricing book and wrote a dollar amount on the card. Then they taped it to the windshield along with a bag of potato chips that bore the note, "The chips are down. We're selling cars for $56 a month." When the owners of these cars returned, they found the "wudjatak" and a dollar amount along with the chips. So many bags of chips were used in the promotion that no one could find potato chips in the stores for days after the campaign began.

The "56 for '56" campaign took off like a flash fire. Lee's office zoomed to first place in sales for Ford. The home office in Detroit took notice of the little Chester office. Suddenly, Lee Iacocca was a very popular, very important employee within the huge Ford Motor Company.

Ford took the "56 for '56" campaign nationwide. The company sold an extra 75,000 cars because of it. It was one of the most successful promotions in the history of the auto business, and it was Lee Iacocca's idea.

The year 1956 was a good one for Lee in other ways, too. For a while it looked as if his romance with Mary would end. They had dated for a rocky seven years, but finally broke up because Mary thought Lee was too attached to his parents and his job to make a very good husband.

Soon after the breakup, Mary became gravely ill and was hospitalized with pneumonia. Lee dropped everything to rush to her side. Her doctors weren't sure she would live, but she passed the crisis in her illness and started to get well. As Mary recovered, her mother convinced her that Lee Iacocca was the only man for her. Mary agreed—she would rather be with Lee than lose him. They became engaged on Mother's Day, and set the wedding date for September 29, 1956.

While Lee and Mary planned their wedding, Lee's success on the job put him in line for a promotion. In July Lee was made manager of the Washington, D.C., district office. But before he could start his new job, Ford gave him a different job in Dearborn, Michigan—the new national truck marketing manager. After ten years of hard work and lots of sweat, Lee was an "overnight success."

When Lee arrived in Dearborn shortly after his marriage, Ford was a much different company than the one founded by Henry Ford I. Lee was promoted partly because of changes that had recently occurred at Ford—changes needed to correct decades of management problems.

Henry Ford started with no money and an idea. From that modest beginning, he built an automobile empire that today stretches around the world. His name and the auto business are so much a part of each other that it is hard to think of one without the other.

Although Henry Ford was the son of a farmer, he loved mechanical things, not animals. After Henry and his father went their separate ways, Henry spent two years tinkering in a shed to build an engine mounted on a four-wheeled vehicle. On June 4, 1896, around three in the morning, he was ready to drive his car for the first time. Then he found that the door to the shed was too small to let him drive through. Not a person to be stopped by such a "minor" problem, Henry chopped down the entire front wall of the shed and drove off in his car. It had no gears and no brakes!

On June 16, 1903, the Ford Motor Company was born. Henry Ford I, like Lee Iacocca, knew what people wanted. Ford once said "I will build a motorcar for the great multitudes. It will be large enough for the family but small enough for individuals to run and care for . . .. But it will be so low in price that no man making a good salary will be unable to own one. . ."

The car, called the Tin Lizzie, or Model T, cost $850. It was the first car built on an assembly line with the steering wheel on the left. By 1912 Henry Ford's plant made 200,000 cars a year. The auto industry was off and running.

While early auto workers earned five dollars for an eight-hour day, Henry Ford was becoming not only famous, but wealthy. He was, in fact, a tempting target for kidnappers.

When Henry discovered a plot to kidnap his son, Edsel, he hired a body guard named Harry Bennett. Bennett was an ex-boxer and ex-sailor. People called him the "Little Fellow," but Bennett never let his five-foot, six-inch height stop him. He could beat men twice his size in a fight, and he often did. Eventually Bennett became Henry's man inside the company. He spied on employees and Henry's family and reported what he learned to Henry. After a while Bennett ran just about everything with total power.

Bennett's power and influence throughout the Ford Motor Company made life hard for many of its employees. Henry's son, Edsel, was the only person who could save the company from Bennett. Edsel, however, was dying of cancer. It would be Edsel's son, Henry Ford II, who would end Bennett's reign of terror at Ford.

Henry Ford II entered the auto business at an early age. When he was three, he lit the blast furnace at the then new River Rouge plant. This was the same plant Lee Iacocca would work in when he began his year of engineering training.

Henry Ford II didn't study very hard in school and college. He married his first wife, Anne, and then went off to fight in World War II. While he was gone, his father Edsel died of cancer. Henry II left the service and returned to Ford to take command of the company. The first problem he had to solve was how to get rid of Bennett.

Henry II arrived at the company with no desk and no office. Bennett was determined to keep the young Ford helpless. Henry II knew very little about the auto business even though he grew up in the world's most powerful auto family. He set out to learn all he could.

The young Ford wandered the plant, asking questions and listening to the answers. He met secretly with executives and officers he knew he could trust. They met at a restaurant outside the plant because they were afraid that Bennett would "bug" their meetings. Nerves were so tense at Ford that people worried a gun battle might break out in the halls.

In 1944, Henry II was made second-in-command next to his grandfather. Bennett, though, was still the most powerful person at Ford. At last Henry II's mother, Eleanor, decided to tip the balance against Bennett.

Eleanor went to see the aging Henry Ford I. She threatened to sell her stock in Ford Motor Company if Henry II was not made president of the company. If she sold her stock, the Ford family would no longer control the company. Since Henry would never allow that to happen, he agreed to Eleanor's demands.

Bennett had lost. He was ordered off the company grounds, and the young Ford took over the day-to-day managing of the auto giant.

Henry II needed strong managers and set about reorganizing the company to bring in bright young people. One of those bright young people was Lee Iacocca. When Lee arrived at the River Rouge plant to begin his engineer training program, the Whiz Kids also arrived.

U.S. Army Air Force officer Charles Bates Thornton

contacted Henry Ford II as World War II ended. Thornton and nine other officers were the best and brightest of experts in a wide range of areas from economics to business management. The ten decided to stay together after the war. They offered Henry II a package deal—if all ten of them were hired by Ford, they would bring to the company the kind of strong, bright management team Henry II needed.

On February 1, 1946, the Whiz Kids arrived. Among them was Robert McNamara, a man who would play a major role in the success of the then-trainee Iacocca. The Whiz Kids spent the first four months at Ford wandering around and asking questions. They asked so many questions that people began calling them the "Quiz Kids."

An era in the auto industry ended in 1947 when Henry Ford I died. Henry II became the head of the company.

When Iacocca was promoted to Dearborn after the "56 for '56" success, Whiz Kid Robert McNamara was vice-president in charge of the Ford division. It was McNamara who recognized Iacocca's selling skills. It was McNamara who took the "56 for '56" campaign nationwide, and it was also under McNamara that Iacocca was made national marketing manager for trucks. McNamara knew that Ford needed people like Lee Iacocca if it was going to survive and succeed.

Chapter / Three

Mr. Mustang

Lee Iacocca moved to Dearborn, near Detroit, without his bride, Mary, and one of his first goals was to find a house. He wanted Mary to join him as soon as possible so that they could live together and set up their own household. Fortunately for Lee, Charles Beacham, his old friend and boss, was also in Dearborn. Beacham helped him find a house. Mary joined him within a month, and Lee could begin concentrating on his job.

As always, Lee began working with his local Ford dealers by going into the field to find out what they needed. He held classes to increase sales, and then put together a special group called a task force to check on sales performance.

Truck sales soared, and Iacocca's future at Ford soared with them. Robert McNamara promoted Lee to marketing manager for cars. When Lee called his dad to share the news, Nick told him to go for the top job.

Lee took his father's advice seriously. Across the country, Ford sales were booming. When registrations of new Fords topped Chevrolet for the first time, Henry Ford II called Iacocca to congratulate him.

Lee's victory was made even sweeter when, a few days later, he and Mary found out that she was pregnant with their first child. It was the one piece of news that made his success on the job fade. Lee and Mary called their families to share the news about the baby and began looking for a bigger house.

While the Iacoccas settled into their new life, Lee made his presence known at Ford. Nick's promotional skills had rubbed off on his son. Lee began to use fancy promotions to bring out and sell new cars. His first chance to demonstrate his promotional skills to Ford executives came soon.

Robert McNamara was preparing to introduce the first American compact car—the Ford Falcon. Iacocca would promote the new car, but both men would be working closely together. Even though McNamara and Iacocca were not at all alike, they respected each other, and their working relationship was a productive, satisfying one.

McNamara believed cars should be useful, and options and luxuries were needed only because they were profitable. He was a "no-nonsense" person and his car, the Falcon, was a "no-nonsense" car. The Falcon had been designed to compete with small imports that had already taken away almost 10 percent of the American car market.

Foreign cars had begun to enter the United States auto

market in the early 1950s. The big carmakers in Detroit didn't think the foreign-made cars, especially the funny looking Volkswagen, were much of a threat to their business. Yet Volkswagen began doubling its sales every year and in 1958 the German car was joined by a Japanese car, Toyota. Detroit began to take notice. Soon the big automakers made plans to draw American car buyers back into the showrooms of the American automakers. McNamara's Falcon was Ford's first answer to foreign cars.

Part of McNamara's no-nonsense approach to his cars was his desire to attract buyers to the Falcon by advertising its safety features. Iacocca disagreed. The saying in Detroit then was "McNamara's selling safety and Chevy's selling cars." Lee had had all the egg on his face he wanted because of auto safety. Safety, Iacocca believed, would appeal only to a small number of car buyers. Instead, he wanted to create a promotion that would make people rush to the showrooms to see and buy the Falcon.

While Iacocca was putting together his plans, Kathi Iacocca was born on June 29, 1959. Lee had a beautiful dark-haired daughter. His family life and his career were moving along nicely, along with the plans for selling the Falcon.

Lee had come up with quite an idea. To make his plan work, he needed an entire town—a small town of about 5,000 people would do. And he found one, Flora, in the heart of Illinois dairy country.

In September 1960, Ford executives drove a parade of Fords into Flora. The Ford Motor Company gave each

family in Flora a 1961 white Falcon, full-size Ford, or
Thunderbird to drive for one week. Truck owners drove a
blue Ford truck. The day the cars arrived, Iacocca went
through the town asking the townspeople how they liked
the cars. Did they want any changes? Was anything
wrong? Reporters flocked to Flora, where Ford officials
encouraged them to ask questions of anyone.

As stories about Flora's Fords appeared in newspapers,
on radio and TV, the publicity made Iacocca a very important person at Ford Motor Company. The Falcon's sales
soared, and McNamara began to think that Iacocca was
one of Ford's most valuable employees. On November 10,
1960, Robert McNamara moved into the president's job at
Ford. At the same time, Lee Iacocca became vice-
president and general manager of the Ford division, the
company's largest section. Iacocca says that when he
became vice-president, half the people in the division didn't
know his name, and the other half couldn't spell it.

Lee began to stamp his new job with his own way of
doing things. He used what was called his "black book."
That meant the people who worked for him had to put
their goals on paper, and they had to determine how well
or how poorly they did every three months. Lee believes
that if you put your goals on paper, it forces you to be honest with yourself about how well you are doing your job.

Lee believes that the best people *act*. They gather as
much information as possible, and then they act, correct-
ing mistakes as they go. Lee could be hard with employees who didn't do their jobs. He wanted his people to do

their best, and he was right there with them, working as hard as he expected them to work. He would not accept excuses from employees who didn't do their best or try their hardest.

While Lee worked as hard as anyone else at Ford, he didn't go out with his staff, and he didn't go to parties with his bosses, especially Henry Ford II. He didn't want to be fired for saying something after he had had a few drinks. Lee always tended to say what he thought, even if his opinion was not popular or pleasant.

In 1960 John F. Kennedy was elected president of the United States, and Robert McNamara accepted the post of secretary of defense in the Kennedy White House. This was one time Lee would not move up behind McNamara. Instead, John Dykstra became president of Ford. Lee, however, was content with his job as head of the Ford division. He loved going to work and was always trying out ideas on the test track.

Lee wanted to design a car that would be popular and would make the company a lot of money. He would have the chance in a few years. In the meantime, he gave the Falcon a classier styling, a convertible top, and a new "promotion." On New Year's Eve, Iacocca loaded two planes with 200 people and flew them to Europe. The new convertible Falcon and 120 reporters went along on the transatlantic trip.

They flew to Monaco, a small country on the coast of the Mediterranean Sea. When they arrived, they went to a New Year's Day party at the palace of the rulers, Prince

Rainier and Princess Grace of Monaco. The Americans toasted the New Year with champagne in beer mugs, and Lee gave the royal family a Ford Thunderbird. Princess Grace received a station wagon for her Red Cross work. Prince Albert, the three-year-old heir to the throne, got a boy-size, handmade Thunderbird.

After the reception, race car drivers gave the U.S. reporters and Ford executives rides in the new Falcon. They had laid out a road-rally course through town and around the surrounding mountains. When Lee Iacocca took his ride with Finnish race driver Timo Makinen, the driver lost control for a minute. The Falcon almost plunged off the road and crashed, but Makinen regained control and finished the run. Iacocca was still shaken as he got out of the car. The Falcon though, had performed beautifully.

Back in the United States, Lee Iacocca had more new ideas to sell Ford cars. In 1961 Iacocca started the "Punt, Pass, and Kick" program with the National Football League. In this program, young people nine to thirteen years old could demonstrate their football skills during halftimes at pro football games. Winners at the local level moved on to district, and then zone, competitions. Champions competed at the Super Bowl halftime.

To sign up, youngsters had to bring a parent or guardian into a Ford dealership. More than 20 million people have visited Ford dealerships to sign up their children for the Punt, Pass, and Kick Program. Many of these parents have looked at new Ford cars while they were there.

1961 was important for another reason. Lee began planning the 1964 cars. In those days it took three years to design and produce a new car—now it may take as long as five or six years.

In order to build a car that will sell, automakers must find out what the public wants. They study what people buy and ask why they buy it. Even something as simple as the color of a car can make it appeal to an entirely different group of people. The baby boomers, an enormous group of young people who were born after World War II, were beginning to reach driving age. Lee wanted a car that would appeal to these young men and women.

Lee put together a group of creative people who met once a week to have dinner and talk. Don Frey, Hal Sperlich, Frank Zimmerman, Walter Murphy, and Sid Olson called themselves the Fairlane Committee. They began to put together the car they wanted to build—a sporty, basic car that offered a variety of options.

Lee says that this time at Ford was his happiest. He and the men he worked with saw their cars as pieces of art—masterpieces. One of those masterpieces was the Mustang, the first car Lee could call his own at Ford.

Iacocca wanted the car to have good performance and be well built to last a long time. He knew that people often bought a car by how it looked, but they were happy with it only if it worked properly. Since the 1964 cars were his alone, Lee would take the credit or the blame for them. He wanted to make sure there would be more credit than blame.

Lee believed the American public was tired of plain economy cars. Ford had started to lose ground to General Motors, the largest company in the auto industry. Iacocca wanted a racy, better performing car than ever before—a car that would fit at the country club, the drag strip, and at church. It had to have a low base price with a number of high-priced options people could choose. To keep the price down, he decided to use some parts made for the Falcon instead of building a completely new car.

Iacocca went directly to Henry Ford II to get approval to develop the new car. Henry threw him out of his office. A week later Iacocca tried again, and an angry Ford again kicked him out. Ford did not want a small car, Iacocca did, and the battle between the two men was on. Iacocca had to convince Ford to approve the car soon since he wanted to bring out the car at the World's Fair in April 1964. To keep that schedule, Lee needed an approved design by September 1, 1962.

An early version of the car was shown to racing car drivers, including Dan Gurney. The drivers loved it. That was a hint to Iacocca that the design was too sporty for the average driver. The designers went back to work. By summer 1962, they still didn't know exactly what the new car would look like. The designers had made eighteen different clay models, but none was right.

Iacocca had only twenty-one months to get Henry Ford's approval, create the final design, choose a plant, get equipment and suppliers, and then arrange for the dealers to sell the car. A design was needed *now*.

The Mustang went through many stages in design before it could be built. The basic design had to be created, and the cost to produce the car estimated. Early models were made in wood and clay. Designers built a full-scale clay model over a wooden frame. The model was worked and reworked until it was exactly right. The front end was covered with chrome, and a dark film was used to look like windshields. The clay model was also tested in a wind tunnel to determine how much air resistance it had—its aerodynamic qualities. Finally metal dies were made for the body parts.

Lee began wearing down Henry's opposition by mentioning the new car whenever he had the chance. Then he held a competition among his designers to come up with a design for the car. The design created by Dave Ash's group was the winner. Even carved out of clay, this design looked like it was on the move. Henry Ford II liked it and gave his approval to go ahead with plans for the new car. Henry, however, wanted an extra inch added to the back seat. Iacocca and his team disagreed because they thought that inch would hurt the looks of the car. Henry refused to give in—either he got his extra inch in the rear or the Mustang would not be built. Lee gave him the extra inch.

Secrecy is important in the auto business. Iacocca fooled the other carmakers by showing off a "fake" car at the American Grand Prix on October 7, 1962. It didn't look enough like the real design to reveal any secrets, but it looked enough like the actual car for Iacocca to see how well it would appeal to the public. Thousands crowded around the Ford display just to see it. They liked what they saw, and Lee knew he was on the right track.

To keep the other automakers confused about what the Mustang really looked like, Iacocca had a second car designed for the 1963 American Grand Prix. Again, racing fans swarmed around the car. Iacocca was sure now that he knew what people wanted, and he was going to give it to them with the Mustang.

The target date to bring out the real car was April 1964, at the World's Fair in New York. On March 9, 1964, the first Mustang rolled off the assembly line. On April 17, dealerships were mobbed with people wanting to see the new car. In Seattle the driver of a cement truck had so much interest in the Mustang in a showroom window that he drove his truck through the plate glass.

Lee Iacocca drove from his home to the office each day in a different Mustang. School children would hang out of school bus windows and shout "Mustang! Mustang! Mustang!" when they saw him go by in the car.

Ford loaned Mustangs to the editors of college newspapers to drive for a few weeks to make a favorable impression on young people. Commercials appeared on television, and colorful ads spread across the pages of magazines.

Iacocca appeared on the covers of both *Time* magazine and *Newsweek*. According to *Time*, "At 39, after 17 years in the auto business, this tall, rugged son of Italian immigrant parents is the hottest young man in Detroit. . ."

Iacocca was called a marketing genius and with good reason. On the first weekend the Mustang appeared in showrooms nationwide, 4 million people went to Ford dealerships to see it.

Soon Mustang clubs formed, and items such as Mustang sunglasses, toys, and key chains were produced. People loved the car's styling and saw it as a "prestige car"—a car that made them look and feel important. The low price helped make it a best seller, especially with standard features such as bucket seats and a three-speed transmission.

Thousands of people wrote to praise the car, and Iacocca read every letter. He heard only one complaint—there weren't enough cars in the showrooms. A dealer in Garland, Texas, auctioned off his only Mustang. The buyer spent the night in the car while his check cleared the bank.

The Mustang stirred the imagination of car buyers from coast to coast. As Mustang "fever" spread, more and more people wanted one of these cars with a revolutionary new look.

To meet the great demand, Ford had to open a second plant in San Jose, California, and even used a third factory to fill orders. The Mustang sold 273,000 cars in nine months. By the end of its first year, 418,812 cars had been sold. Iacocca had broken the record McNamara made with the Falcon. The press began to call him "Mr. Mustang"—a name that would last for more than twenty years.

The Mustang wasn't the only Iacocca creation to appear in 1964. His second daughter, Lia, was born that summer. And if that wasn't enough, in 1964 the Ford Motor Company returned to the race car circuit. Lee Iacocca was behind the wheel there, too.

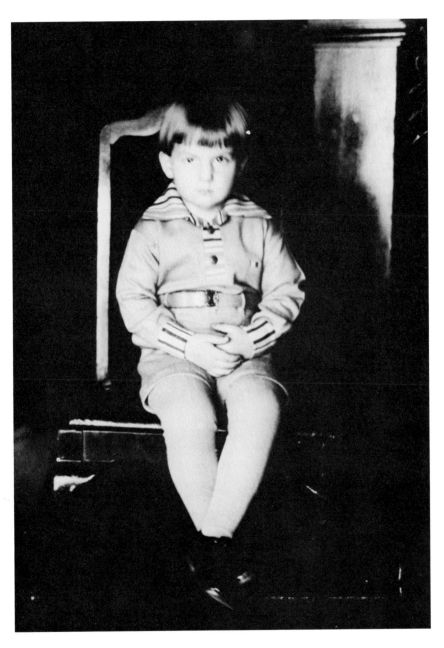

As a young boy, Lee Iacocca posed for this photograph.

This portrait of Lee Iacocca was taken when he was a young Ford Motor Company executive.

Robert McNamara, then a top Ford executive, discusses business with Henry Ford II.

Lee Iacocca listens to Henry Ford II at a meeting of the company's shareholders—the people who own Ford Motor Company stock.

Twenty years after the Mustang first appeared, Lee Iacocca had this framed sculpture of the original car on the wall of his office.

(Above) *The Iacoccas posed for this family portrait when Lee was president of Ford: Mary and Lee* (top) *and Kathi and Lia* (bottom). (Opposite page) *A close-up view of Lee Iacocca at a U.S. Senate hearing.*

*Lee Iacocca with Douglas Fraser, then president of the
United Auto Workers—the union representing American
auto workers.*

Chapter/Four

The Mustang had shown I was someone to watch

Lee Iacocca was the man to watch at Ford. He was moving as fast as the Mustang. If you look at the Mustang emblem on the car's grille, you will see that the horse runs clockwise. Since American race horses run counterclockwise, this Mustang was a runaway—in more ways than one. The other automakers had to run very hard to catch up with it.

Creating the plans for the Mustang, and preparing for the birth of his second daughter, weren't the only things Lee was doing. Henry Ford II wanted his company to build a race car that would beat the best of the famous Italian automaker, Ferrari.

Ever since the head of Ferrari, Enzo Ferrari, had refused to sell his company to Ford, Henry wanted revenge. And he wanted that revenge on the race track. He ordered Lee Iacocca to build a race car that would defeat Ferrari's best. Lee eagerly rose to meet the challenge because he believed that auto racing sold cars. People watched auto races and wanted to buy the cars that were winners. If Ford cars won, and cars with Ford engines won, the public would want to buy Fords.

Ford cars and engines began challenging the stars of the race track. In June 1964, a Ford GT40 with a 4.2 liter V8 engine became the first American car to race against the Europeans at the LeMans Grand Prix in France. Ford lost, but Henry swore to return and win at the 1965 LeMans. He ordered Lee to put together a car that would do it.

Iacocca put his racing team to work. At the next LeMans, in practice sessions, the Ford car lapped 5.1 seconds faster than the Ferrari cars. Still, Ferrari won the race and embarrassed Henry Ford II again. Ford demanded that Iacocca get the racing cars ready for the 1966 LeMans race. Henry did not want to be embarrassed again, and he wasn't since Ford cars took first, second, and third place in that race. Not satisfied, Henry ordered Iacocca to do it again the next year.

As Lee tackled the problem of building a race car that would win, the Mustang roared onto roads all over America and around the world. Ford hit a new sales record worldwide, and Iacocca's division made up 75 percent of the sales. The Mustang's success earned him a promotion to vice-president of the corporate car and truck group. He moved his office into the Ford headquarters building called the Glass House—a twelve-story rectangle of unbroken reflective glass. There Lee joined a group of executives that ate lunch with Henry Ford II each day.

Lee Iacocca was now only a few steps from being made president of Ford Motor Company.

The executives in the Glass House were treated like royalty. The executive cafeteria, where chefs imported food from around the world, was like one of the country's finest restaurants. Diners could order anything they wanted, but Henry Ford II always had a hamburger made of ground New York steak.

Life at the Glass House kept up a tense, high-pressure, fast-paced schedule of meetings to attend and tough decisions to make. Lee's family life, though, provided a refuge for him. In the Iacocca house life was friendly and relaxed, and there were often guests around the dinner table. The Iacoccas were happiest at home with friends and family around them.

Mary, however, suffered from diabetes, a disease that requires its victims to watch everything they eat. Sometimes they lose consciousness and go into a coma. That condition is like fainting, but much more dangerous.

Mary's disease became worse after Lia was born. She was often rushed to the hospital unconscious. Whenever she fell ill, Lee rushed home from meetings. He went with her to the doctor for tests and treatments and made sure his friends looked after her when he was out of town on business. Lee worried about Mary since she was everything to him—his wife, best friend, and lifetime companion.

Despite Mary's illness, Lee believes that she was stronger than him in many ways. Once when Kathi fell off her bike, the girl suffered a bad head injury. Lee fainted and Mary took charge, taking their daughter to the hospital. After she made sure Kathi was all right, she went home and took care of Lee. Another time when their friend Bill Winn had a heart attack, Mary called the rescue team while Lee panicked.

Lee needed the support and love of his family to help him carry the responsibilities of his job. He was tackling a wide range of projects and problems. While Iacocca was working on the company's racing fleet, he was also working on selling the cars made by the Lincoln/Mercury division.

In September 1966, Iacocca took his dealers to sea on the luxury liner *SS Independence.* On the second night out from New York, the crew released a mountain of helium balloons from the ship's deck. The 1967 Mercury Marquis, a full size luxury car, was hidden underneath them. But that wasn't all.

When the ship docked at Charlotte Amalie in the American Virgin Islands, Iacocca hosted an evening luau—a beachside dinner of barbecued ribs and chicken. Five hundred torches lit up the night. A World War II landing craft, covered with leaves and banana stalks, appeared at sea. After it beached itself in front of the dealers, a white luxury sports car rolled out onto a stage. Lights blazed on it, and singer Vic Damone stepped out to introduce the 1967 Cougar.

The Cougar took off in the steps of the Mustang. Before long, the "sign of the cat"—the Cougar perched on the Lincoln/Mercury sign—became the symbol for the entire Lincoln/Mercury division.

When Iacocca returned home, he turned to the advertising for the Mercury cars. He wanted to prove to the public that the Mercury Marquis had a better ride than its competitors. He used a series of now-famous commercials showing just how smooth a ride the car had. In one commercial the car was driven with a bottle of nitroglycerin in the back seat. Nitroglycerin is an explosive that can easily blow up if its container is shaken too hard. To prove that the nitroglycerin was real, technicians blew up the car at the end of the commercial.

The most famous commercial showed a diamond cutter with a large precious gem. He sat in the back seat of a car being driven over a very rough road. As the car bounced over the road, the diamond cutter cut the gem without damaging it. The commercial became so well known that the performers of "Saturday Night Live" later spoofed it on their program.

On the race track, however, success was not so easy. Although Ford had some of racing's finest drivers, the 1967 LeMans event started out badly when three out of the four Fords that were entered in the race crashed. The fourth Ford, driven by the Dan Gurney and A.J. Foyt team, finally took the lead with two Ferraris close behind. A short while later, the two Ferraris passed Gurney. He slammed the accelerator to the floor and kept it there, passing the Ferraris and crossing the finish line more than thirty miles ahead of them. Ford won for the second year in a row, but troubles at home would prevent the company from entering another European race.

In the United States and abroad, 1967 was a violent year. Summer race riots destroyed the peace of Detroit. Whole neighborhoods went up in flames. Overseas, Ford products were banned in Arab countries because Ford had a plant in Israel and the Arabs and Israelis were fighting. Since Ford cars had been popular in Arab countries, the company lost large numbers of sales. Also in 1967, Ford recalled one-third of its cars for repairs of badly made vehicles. It paid a quarter of a million dollars in postage alone to tell owners about the recalls.

Despite these problems, Lee and many others believed he was the most likely person to become the next president of Ford. Henry Ford II, though, wanted Iacocca to get more experience. Henry passed over Lee and went outside the company for its next president.

At General Motors, Ford's biggest competitor in Detroit, Bunkie Knudsen had also been passed over for president. Bunkie was a seasoned, sharp auto man. His father had been president of General Motors, and now Bunkie was looking for a new job. Henry leaped at the chance to get him to come to Ford.

Since Lee was on a skiing trip with his family when Bunkie accepted Ford's job offer, Henry sent a DC3 airplane to bring Lee home. Iacocca was terribly disappointed. He was eager to become number one at Ford, and he felt tempted to leave the company over the hiring of Knudsen. Yet he stayed, believing that one day the presidency would be his. Soon it looked as if he might not have long to wait.

Knudsen clashed with Iacocca by being the same kind of high-powered manager that Iacocca was. Lee resented Bunkie's power, and their feuding became a barely concealed war in the halls of Ford Motor Company. As soon as Knudsen gave employees orders, Iacocca would come along and change the orders.

Bunkie also didn't have many loyal friends or employees at the company. He was never really accepted there since many at Ford considered him an outsider. Knudsen interfered with daily running of the company too much, making changes without asking either Ford or Iacocca.

Iacocca, on the other hand, surrounded himself with persons he could trust such as Gar Laux, Hal Sperlich, and Frank Zimmerman. He also had Henry Ford II's brother and mother on his side, which gave him real power inside the company. Iacocca set out to use that power. He would prove that he, not Bunkie, was the one who should head the Ford Motor Company.

Lee decided to introduce a new luxury car based on a popular car of the 1930s, the Mark. During the 1950s, Ford had brought out the Mark II, and both cars were considered classics. Lee revived the Mark line with the Mark III, a two-seat sportscar the size of a limousine. When it came out in April 1968, it outsold the Cadillac Eldorado, then the leading two-door luxury car. "The Mustang had shown I was someone to watch," Lee writes in his autobiography. "The Mark III made it clear I was no flash in the pan. I was forty-four, Henry Ford had taken me under his wing, and my future never looked better."

Bunkie Knudsen remained president for only nineteen months. One day Henry Ford II walked into Knudsen's office and told him he no longer had a job at Ford. After Bunkie was fired, Lee wondered if the same fate was in store for him sometime in the future. He talked to Mary about leaving the company, but once more decided to stay.

With Knudsen gone, Lee should have been the next Ford president. Instead, Henry Ford II put together a three-man team with Robert J. Hampson and Robert Stevenson as copresidents with Iacocca. Henry began talking to the press about bringing his son into the company. Once again, Lee wondered if he should leave, but he didn't. From within Ford and from outside the company, he had to deal with many problems and challenges.

In 1966 the U.S. National Highway Safety Board was created, and in January 1968, it began issuing national automobile safety standards. The American public was concerned about pollution and had put pressure on politicians to pass laws to protect the environment. These government standards for auto exhaust emissions and safety could not be met without adding to the cost of making cars. Lee Iacocca worried that the added costs would hurt sales of Ford cars.

The growing sales of foreign cars were also cutting into Ford's share of the auto market. In 1969 sales of compact, front-wheel drive foreign cars topped one million for the first time. More and more people were buying imports because they were well made and used less gasoline than domestic models. Iacocca wanted to be making cars that could compete with imports, but Henry Ford II did not want to invest the research money needed to develop such automobiles.

Lee had to settle for the Pinto, the first U.S.-made sub-compact car designed for people with modest incomes. The Pinto was unveiled at the Las Vegas convention center. In front of 2,000 auto dealers, a "flying saucer" hovered over the stage. It landed in a cloud of smoke and lifted off to reveal a bright yellow Pinto.

The dealers believed that the Pinto would be Ford's biggest seller since the Mustang. They were right—the company sold more than 250,000 Pintos in the first twelve months. Lee Iacocca, it appeared, had earned his reputation as the father of the small car.

Meanwhile, back in the Glass House, Henry Ford II's three-man team wasn't working very well. Since all three men reported directly to Henry, he found himself too involved in the daily running of the company. By December 1970, he had decided to make Iacocca Ford's only president. Iacocca, however, had received some attractive offers from other companies. He showed one particularly good one to Henry. In order to stay with Ford, Lee demanded and received a long term contract.

Lee called Mary, and then his parents who flew out to help him celebrate. His office was now next to Henry's, but the president's chair at Ford was a hot seat. While the

men who sat there usually didn't last long, Iacocca didn't
see himself that way. He loved his job even though it was
tough.

Although Lee worked hard in his new job, he found
the time to call home every day and to call his parents
every weekend. Friday night was his poker night, and
weekends were spent with his family. As practicing Cath-
olics, the Iacoccas attended Mass as a family. They spent
most holidays and other special days at home.

When Lee made a promise to his family, he kept it.
Once, his schedule got mixed up, and a meeting with
Henry Ford II was set for the same time he had promised
to go on an outing with his children. Lee refused to cancel
his date with his daughters. He went with them instead of
attending the company meeting.

Lee Iacocca was a family man all the way. He didn't
like fancy parties and jet set people. Instead, he preferred
to have friends over for a casual dinner of Mary's home-
made pasta. His den, called "Lido's Lounge," was
equipped with a movie projector, stereo system, game
table, and items he valued from his life. It was his think
tank. Lee often sat in the den and listened to jazz music as
he made plans for the company.

Lee Iacocca now had huge responsibilities. Ford
Motor Company had more than 400,000 employees. It
built 2.5 million cars and 750,000 trucks a year in North
America alone. Not only did Iacocca have to make sure
Ford cars sold, but he had to find ways to cut costs and
increase profits. Lee started a "shuck the losers" program.

Managers had three years to make sure their department made a profit or it would be sold.

Iacocca expected the best from his staff and encouraged them to keep reaching for even higher goals. Above all, Lee Iacocca believes in honesty. According to his old friend, Leo-Arthur Kelmenson, Iacocca wants people to stand up for what they believe in, and then prove what they believe in is right.

His longtime friends—Gar Laux, Bill Winn, Hal Sperlich—think of Iacocca as one of their most loyal associates. Some people, however, believe you have to be one of Iacocca's friends to be treated well. They say he could ignore you if he didn't like you, and he sometimes kept people waiting outside his office after he agreed to see them.

People who have worked with him say Iacocca is a tough man to please and makes hard demands on his staff. An article in *Time* magazine once described Iacocca as "a tough-talking and demanding executive. . .who usually remains secluded in his office with his door firmly shut. . ."

According to Mary Iacocca, "Some of the men he works with call him the Iron Chancellor. . .at the office, but around the house, he's a lamb. He calls Kathi 'Olive Oyl' and Lia 'Sweet Pea.' They call him 'Wimpy.'"

Tough manager or not, fair with his employees or not, Lee Iacocca now managed one of the world's largest automakers. There was nowhere to move. The top job, the man who would replace Henry Ford II, would be a member of the Ford family. Henry had made it clear that there would always be a Ford in charge of the company.

Despite his powerful job, trouble lay ahead for Lee Iacocca. He was headed for the biggest fall of his life, and Ford's new small car, the Pinto, would play a part in it.

Chapter/Five

The bigger you are, the harder you fall

In 1972 the fuel tanks of Pintos began to explode in rear-end collisions, killing and injuring passengers and drivers. Lawsuits piled up as fiery accidents took lives and left horribly scarred victims.

The courts believed that Ford Motor Company did not take enough care in developing a safe car. In the rush to get the car ready, and meet the production deadlines Iacocca had set, mistakes may have occurred in the construction of the final car. Even though the company had conducted tests of both front and rear collisions, and even though there had been gas tank ruptures, Ford officials did not recognize the seriousness of the problem. The Pinto gas tank was linked to two dozen deaths, $60 million in lawsuits, and 1.4 million recalls of faulty cars.

This was also a time of personal sadness for Lee Iacocca. His father died while Lee was developing the Mustang II. Lee was heartbroken. He flew home to be with his mother, and then buried his grief by concentrating on his job.

Working on the Mustang II helped Lee cope with his grief. The new car came out on September 21, 1973. From the beginning, though, it didn't have a chance to succeed.

On October 19, 1973, Arab countries cut off oil shipments to the United States because of U.S. support for Israel in the latest Arab-Israeli war. Iacocca knew Ford needed small cars to meet the challenge. The best selling imports were Japanese and German models. Not only were these cars small and efficient, they were well made and well priced.

Lee finally persuaded Henry Ford II to create a small, fuel efficient car in Europe to be called the Fiesta. It took three years to develop and produce.

More problems with Ford cars appeared in 1974. The company was fined $3.5 million by the federal government because some employees had cheated on auto exhaust emission-control tests. These tests were required by the 1970 Clean Air Act to help control air pollution. Henry Ford II and Lee Iacocca were furious when they discovered what their employees were doing. The company pleaded guilty to the charges and paid the fines.

Iacocca had other problems inside Ford Motor Company. Henry Ford II was always called Mr. Ford, even by Iacocca, and he took his role as head of the company seriously. Special equipment in his office gave him information on more than a thousand executives. Henry, though, often didn't do his own dirty work. He had Iacocca do it. It fell to Iacocca to fire executives Henry wanted out of the company. Henry even ordered him to fire his own friends.

Iacocca was on a tour of the Middle East when Henry Ford II cut $2 billion out of his budget. It included the money to develop new small cars and cars with front wheel drive.

Lee was angry. General Motors and Chrysler were working hard to produce small cars, and Lee wanted Ford to compete with them in this important area. Iacocca believed that Ford should switch to small, fuel efficient cars. He wanted the company to plan a front wheel drive car that could appeal to the buyers of German and Japanese imports. Iacocca and Sperlich came up with a plan, but Henry said no. Henry believed it was too risky a venture.

In 1975, Ford Motor Company announced its first loss since 1946. Henry Ford II began to get chest pains, which sometimes signal a heart attack. When Henry became ill, his brother, William Clay Ford, agreed to take his place if he could leave the day-to-day running of the company to someone else. That worried Henry. He wanted to make sure his company would always be run by a member of the Ford family. Since his own son, Edsel, was too young to take such a responsibility, that left an outsider—Lee Iacocca.

When the Fiesta, Ford's new small car, appeared in the United States, it sold so well that Henry Ford began to resent Iacocca. Ford loved Europe, and the Fiesta was

Ford's European car. According to Iacocca, the Ford name, power, and money meant something in Europe. Since Henry Ford considered Europe to be his territory, he was annoyed by Iacocca's success with the Fiesta.

In Henry's eyes, Lee Iacocca was becoming too popular. He was also becoming one of the company's most powerful presidents. Under Iacocca's leadership, the company made record profits and sales. The board of directors, most company executives, and the Ford dealers all liked and respected him. His popularity was a threat to Henry Ford's desire that a Ford would always run the company.

Henry thought that Iacocca had become too self-important. He began teasing Lee about going to church and being a good family man. Iacocca took the teasing with outward calm, but inside he was angered by such insulting and personal comments. Lee believed Henry was out to force him to resign. And it did seem as if Henry was out to get rid of him—especially when strange things began to happen.

Iacocca's secretary told him that every time he made a telephone call on the company credit card, Ford received a record of it. She had also noticed that papers on Lee's desk were moved during the night. Finally Lee learned that Henry had started a probe—an investigation of his private and business life. He was furious and almost resigned to protest Henry's actions. Yet he decided to stay because he was afraid he would look guilty even though he had done nothing improper or illegal.

Much of the probe centered on a limousine and travel agency owned by a friend of Iacocca's, Bill Fugazy. Henry believed that suppliers such as Fugazy were giving Ford executives kickbacks—money and gifts in return for business.

Lee refused to believe Henry could be right. Fugazy was an old and dear family friend who came from a leading New York family. Fugazy says that during the probe his phones were tapped and his office files were taken and not returned for months. At last Iacocca began to realize that Fugazy wasn't the real target of the probe—he was.

Henry had employees of Ford suppliers questioned. His investigators probed Iacocca's friends, purchases, investments, how he entertained. They conducted more than 500 interviews.

Iacocca began leaving the Glass House to make phone calls, and he found himself talking in whispers. He heard stories of wiretaps, bugged phones and rooms, and stolen papers. Then, suddenly, the probe was stopped. Lee Iacocca and his friends had done nothing wrong.

The probe cost Ford $1.5 million. According to Iacocca, Henry Ford wanted something he could use against him to keep him in his place, but Iacocca had nothing to hide. His life was clean. When Ford couldn't get him, Iacocca says, he decided to punish Lee's innocent friend, Bill Fugazy. Fugazy's contract with Ford was cancelled, and Ford made Iacocca do the dirty work. Lee had to call Fugazy to tell him. Although the cancelled

contract cost the New York supplier $2 million, Bill
Fugazy felt sorrier for Lee.

Hal Sperlich was the next person to be fired. When he
left Ford, he went to Chrysler. The loss of Sperlich at
Ford was deeply felt by Iacocca. Sperlich had played a
major role in the creation of the Mustang, the Fiesta, and
many other cars. Iacocca thought Sperlich was the best
auto executive in Detroit.

Despite the constant problems and pressures, Lee
Iacocca decided to stay at Ford Motor Company. He had
spent his entire working life at Ford, and he enjoyed being
president. He liked the power and the prestige and
believed his situation would improve. Yet life at Ford
finally became too hard to bear. Lee told friends he
planned to quit in October 1979, after his fifty-fifth birthday. Henry Ford II, however, wasn't going to wait for
Iacocca to make the move to leave. Ford began applying
pressure.

In 1977 Henry removed some of Iacocca's power by
creating a three-person office of the chief executive.
Henry Ford II was the chairperson and chief executive
officer; Phil Caldwell, the vice-chairperson; and Lee
Iacocca, the president.

Caldwell was now number two and Iacocca number
three in the company. The move reduced Iacocca's power
and control. Lee handled the change well even though he
was boiling inside. He defended the decision to the public
and the press, while revealing his real feelings only to his
family and friends. Lee thought the three-way team was a

three-headed monster that would keep anyone from making any decisions.

Lee says now that he should have quit his job at Ford then. His love for the company and his $970,000 a year income kept him from leaving. Later Lee said, "It might have been pride, it might have been stupidity, but I was not going to crawl out of there with my tail between my legs."

The longer Lee stayed, the more pressure Henry applied to force him to leave. Iacocca was dropped another step when Henry brought William Clay Ford, his younger brother, into the management team to keep power in the Ford family. Now Lee was number four. To make things worse, no one told him about the change until just before it was announced. Iacocca now reported to Caldwell.

On June 12, 1978, Henry met with the nine outside members of Ford's board of directors. He told them he was going to fire Iacocca, but the board refused to allow him to do so. Henry refused to give up. One month later he told the board that either Iacocca went or he did. Faced with that unfortunate choice, the board gave him its approval to fire Iacocca.

That night Iacocca was home when he got a call from the publisher of *Automotive News*. The publisher asked him if the "rumor" was true. Iacocca guessed what he meant. Lee was upset and angry, but he kept his feelings hidden the next day at the office. All day Iacocca waited. That afternoon he was called to Henry's office.

Henry and William Clay Ford were at a marble conference room table. Henry told Lee that he was reorganizing
the company, and it would be best if Iacocca left. Henry
never told Lee directly that he was fired.

Lee refused to turn and leave. He wanted to make
Henry squirm and demanded to know why he was being
fired. Iacocca reminded Ford of all he had done for the
company, the profits his cars had made, but Henry refused
to budge.

The meeting lasted forty-five minutes. When it was
over, so was Iacocca's career at Ford. In one day Lee
Iacocca went from president of one of the world's most
powerful companies to an unemployed man.

"They say that the bigger you are, the harder you fall,"
Lee said later. "Well, I fell a great distance that week. I
instantly identified with every person I had ever fired."

The auto industry was stunned. The *New York Times*
wrote that Iacocca's firing was "one of the most dramatic
shakeups in the history of the Ford Motor Company."
Veteran TV journalist Walter Cronkite said the events at
Ford looked like the plot of a novel. But this was no novel.
This was real.

Lee's younger daughter Lia called him from tennis
camp in tears. She had heard about his firing on the radio
and wanted to know why he hadn't warned the family. He
told her he had had no chance to warn them because
Henry hadn't given him any warning. Even worse for Lee,
his wife, Mary, had her first heart attack three months
after he was fired.

Lee wonders how he could have protected his family better than he did. For the two years before the firing, Lee had not told his family everything that was going on at Ford. They didn't realize how bad the situation had been. Lee hadn't told them because he wanted to protect them.

Sadly for Lee and his family, not all of his friends supported him. Some of the other executives at Ford were nervous and worried about their own jobs. For some people, Iacocca no longer existed—they didn't want to be seen with him and didn't call him. They were afraid of being fired if Henry found out they were in touch with Lee. One of his best friends at Ford, someone he had known for twenty-five years, never even called him after he was fired. They had played poker together, had gone on vacations together, but the man acted as if Lee had died.

"After July 13, 1978," writes Victor Lasky in his book about Henry Ford, "those who admired Lee Iacocca and wished to remain in the employ of Henry Ford learned to keep it to themselves."

Lee found it hard to accept the way his friends at Ford now treated him. Mary was crushed by the way their friends abandoned them. Lee's daughter Kathi says, "He'll always be mad at Henry Ford. He will take it to his grave."

The publicity was the worst Henry Ford II had ever received. Rumors flew about why Iacocca had been fired. Some people thought Ford and Iacocca had clashed because of their backgrounds. Ford came from an old, wealthy family. Iacocca, while not poor, was the son of immigrant parents. Henry's family was loose-knit; Iacocca's was close. Henry was outgoing and could be very friendly. Iacocca was less outgoing and could be highly protective of his privacy. Others thought that Henry had resented Lee's popularity at Ford. Only Henry Ford II knows the real reason, and he has not made it public.

Critics of Iacocca claim he was not as good a manager as he has been given credit for in TV reports and newspaper and magazine articles. Ford designers claim that Iacocca "stole" the Mustang by claiming responsibility for its creation when all he really did was sell the car to the public. "The model was totally completed by the time Lee saw it," says retired Ford design director Gene Bordinat.

Iacocca has also been criticized for his stand on certain safety issues. Even though he has always been a strong supporter of requiring car passengers to wear seat belts, some Ford workers claim he did not always respond to other safety needs. That was especially true, say these workers, if the safety questions threatened his production schedule or the design of the car. For instance, Lee was determined to produce the Pinto for a price of less than $2,000 and a weight of less than 2,000 pounds. When Ford engineers discovered that adding weight to the Pinto fuel tank would protect it, but would also delay production, no one wanted to tell Iacocca the news.

The Pinto problems weren't over. Shortly after Iacocca left Ford, the National Highway Safety Administration had pushed for a recall of all 1971–76 Pintos.

Before the U.S. government could act, Ford voluntarily recalled 1.37 million Pintos and 3,000 Bobcats (the Mercury version of the Pinto). The problems with the Pinto—one of Iacocca's cars—began to cause doubts about all Ford automobiles. Since Lee Iacocca was president during the time these cars were made, he must take some responsibility for the problems and reputation Ford cars had when he left the company.

There were technical matters to resolve before Iacocca could leave Ford. He and the company agreed to let the record show Iacocca resigned as of October 15, 1978, on his fifty-fourth birthday. During the next ninety days, they would put together his financial settlement. The day after the firing, Lee was given a desk in a tiny space in the Ford auto parts plant on Telegraph Road. Reporters were waiting for him as he arrived at his new office, and the public shame was almost more than he could bear. Within an hour, Lee left and set up his office at home. He never came back.

Iacocca's settlement gave him $1 million a year through 1980. There was one hitch, however. He could not go to work for another automobile company. At first that was all right with Lee since he looked forward to relaxing for a while. He could take his time deciding what to do with the rest of his life.

Lee could retire, since his retirement benefits were more than $175,000 a year. But he ". . . really didn't want to retire. I really didn't want to be banished from the auto scene."

Lee began to receive job offers within days of his firing by Ford. Two business schools offered him the position of dean. Charles Tandy, owner of Tandy Corporation, asked him to work for his company. Lee wasn't interested in these offers, though. More than anything else, he wanted to make cars, and he had to be in the car business to be truly happy.

While Iacocca and Ford were playing out their drama, Chrysler, another major U.S. auto company, was in serious trouble. Iacocca's firing gave John Riccardo, head of Chrysler Corporation, a tremendous chance to save his company. Iacocca was an auto genius, and Chrysler needed him. In August Riccardo called Iacocca. They agreed to meet.

Chapter/Six

*The glue that held
the Chrysler Corporation
together*

The meetings between Iacocca and Chrysler were secret
to keep them from being reported by the news media. Lee
often met Chrysler officials at the Waldorf-Astoria Hotel
in New York. Iacocca would take the elevator to the
thirty-fourth floor where Ford had a suite. He would then
walk up two flights to the Chrysler suite.

Taking on the job of saving Chrysler would ruin
Iacocca's reputation if he failed. Yet if he succeeded, it
would avenge his firing by Henry Ford—and save one of
the largest and best known American auto companies.

Next to Henry Ford I, Walter Chrysler, the founder of
Chrysler, was the auto industry's most important member.
In 1908, Chrysler bought an early car called the Locomobile. He took it apart and put it back together again. Then
he went to work for the American Locomobile Works as a
plant engineer. Afterward, Chrysler worked for several auto
companies, always moving toward his dream of having his

own company. He founded the Chrysler Corporation in 1925, and in 1928 he merged Dodge into the company.

Chrysler was an engineering genius. Like Iacocca, he was a strong marketing person, and he even appeared in Chrysler's ads. When Chrysler died in 1940, the company was number two behind General Motors. By the time Iacocca arrived, though, the company was in deep trouble.

At that time Chrysler concentrated so much on low to medium priced cars that they were called "miser motors." These types of cars don't make much of a profit for an auto company. As a result, Chrysler didn't have enough money to handle the tough years when car sales were down. Starting in the mid-1970s, Chrysler lost millions of dollars. It needed new plants and equipment but didn't have the money to build them or buy them. Chrysler needed Lee Iacocca's management abilities and his knowledge of the auto industry.

Lee wanted to know exactly where Chrysler was and where it was going. The picture was bad, but he thought he could turn it around. No one, not even Chrysler executives, knew how bad it was.

By October the deal between Iacocca and Chrysler looked like it could work. Because Lee would lose $1.5 million in settlement money from Ford, Chrysler "bought out" his contract so he would not lose the money. Lee also wanted to be the top executive at Chrysler.

At first Iacocca would work as "Mr. Inside." That meant he would handle the day-to-day affairs of the company, and Riccardo would be "Mr. Outside" to handle relations with Congress and the banks. Iacocca would be chief operating officer for one year. Then Riccardo would retire, and Lee would take his job too.

When Lee's new job with Chrysler was announced, he said, "I really believe that if we can turn this company around then I will have capped a career. I will have helped 200,000 people in their livelihoods. We are the biggest private employer in Detroit. I would have helped the city. They won't know it, but I will have helped GM and Ford compete more."

Privately, he told his good friend, Bill Fugazy, "It's one hell of a challenge." Iacocca would need all of his courage and skill to face the years ahead.

Lee met with the Chrysler officers about a week after accepting the job. Riccardo listed the problems at the troubled company. Iacocca was shocked at how bad things were. "Everybody had his own little empire," Lee said later. "Twenty little companies and nobody to pull them together."

Engineering and purchasing were run by one company manager. Manufacturing, which is related to purchasing, was run by another manager who also ran the sales and marketing departments. To make things even worse, one department didn't know what another was doing. An engineer would come up with a great idea but didn't know if manufacturing could build it.

Chrysler had a huge number of unsold cars sitting in open-air lots. They accounted for millions of dollars in costs for production and storage space. That didn't include the costs for damaged paint, broken windows, and slashed tires the cars suffered in the lots. A recall of 1978 models was also draining the company's remaining funds. In fact, Chrysler was running out of money.

The company reported the worst loss in its history. Lee believed that Chrysler didn't make money because it spent money in all the wrong ways.

Three weeks after Iacocca arrived, he reorganized the company and promoted Hal Sperlich. Iacocca knew he could rebuild his executive team using Sperlich as a base. He brought in three retired Ford executives—Hans Matthias for quality control, Paul Bergmoser for purchasing, and Gar Laux for the dealers. Improving quality was the key to Iacocca's plan. He knew people kept buying a particular car because of its quality, and they stopped buying it if its quality was poor. Purchasing was also important because manufacturers must be able to get the most for the least amount of money to make a profit. The dealers were vital to automakers because they actually sell the cars to the public.

To help build his team, Iacocca brought a number of active Ford executives to Chrysler. Luckily for him, William Clay Ford gave him permission to take his black notebooks with him when he left Ford. Iacocca used those notebooks to identify and hire talented people away from Ford. Over the next three years, he would fire thirty-three of Chrysler's thirty-five vice-presidents. Iacocca hated the firings. Since he had learned the hard way what it meant to lose a job, he tried to put himself in the other person's shoes and be as kind as possible.

Chrysler dealers often had problems getting the cars their customers ordered on time. Iacocca called a meeting of the Chrysler Dealer Council, a committee of dealers, and asked for their complaints. Then two weeks later he had the Chrysler dealers from all over the country meet. Iacocca explained the company's problems and made it clear some hard times lay ahead for everyone at Chrysler. He told them their meeting was the first step on the road to success, and then introduced the 1980 line of cars.

Iacocca acted like a football coach urging his team from behind. He told the dealers a story about Vince Lombardi's three-point formula for winning—talent, discipline, and caring for each other. He compared Chrysler's problems to the fourth quarter of a Super Bowl when the only thing keeping players going is their feelings for their fellow players. The dealers loved the story, and they loved Lee Iacocca. But mutual admiration would not be able to stem the flow of worldwide problems that were about to send the auto industry into a tailspin.

On January 16, 1979, the Shah and ruler of Iran, Mohammed Reza Pahlavi, fled his country. That set into motion events even Lee Iacocca couldn't control. The revolution in Iran caused a cutback in the country's oil production. Since gasoline is made from oil, the result was a gas shortage and high fuel prices. Gas stations began closing, and those that remained open began rationing— allowing a certain amount to each customer. Suddenly, people wanted small cars that didn't use much gas, just the kind Japan and Germany were selling. The demand for foreign cars skyrocketed, and American auto companies didn't have the products needed to compete with the imports.

Iacocca had to cope with these worldwide events in addition to solving the problems within Chrysler. While he struggled to bring the company under control, Riccardo visited more than eighty banks in spring 1979. He met with officials of every major European bank to get them to grant new loans and keep paying old loans. He went to every U.S. government department and agency in Washington, D.C., for help. Iacocca, on his side, began to cut, cut, cut expenses.

By September, Riccardo decided to step aside early, and Iacocca took over the entire company. It became clear that Chrysler was desperate. The company was losing money daily. Chrysler closed plants that were draining funds, sold the division that built tanks, and got rid of much of the property the company owned. The company fired people who weren't needed or who weren't doing their jobs. According to Iacocca, the firings were some of the most painful actions he had to take to save the company.

The only way for Chrysler to stay in business was quick aid from the U.S. government. Some people thought Chrysler should declare bankruptcy—say it couldn't pay its debts and seek legal protection—rather than ask the government for help. But Congress would consider loan guarantees—a promise to pay back bank loans given to the company—if Chrysler put together a plan to make the company healthy again.

Iacocca went to Congress over and over to answer questions about the company. For hours and days, he responded to tough questions from committee members. It was like being on trial. There would be no broken eggs with this performance. Iacocca pointed out that loan guarantees had been granted to railroads, shipbuilders, airlines, and electric companies. Chrysler wasn't the first company to need them.

If the loan guarantees were granted, said Iacocca, Chrysler would have the money it needed to survive. That would save jobs—many thousands of them. It would keep suppliers working. If Chrysler collapsed, it would cost the United States $2.7 billion in the first year alone for unemployment and welfare payments. Lee tried to make Congress think of the guarantees not so much as money and risk, but in human terms—as lost jobs and families suffering hardships. Iacocca told Congress, "People make companies. I think we are doing enough to help ourselves. You just watch us. You will see a lot of action at Chrysler. You will see better cars and you will see better service and better quality. And that, in the end, is all that is going to matter."

Iacocca went to Washington two or three times a week. Auto dealers and union leaders came to Congress to tell their representatives what it would mean if Chrysler went bankrupt. They gained the support of President

Jimmy Carter and Speaker of the House of Representatives, Tip O'Neill.

Iacocca was also trying to run Chrysler. He had eight or ten meetings a day, and all the activity and worries began to affect him in strange ways. "I'd wake up in the middle of the night. My mind never got settled. I worked twenty-four hours a day. I can't describe it, but I'd be less than honest if I didn't say there was a three-month period where you'd wonder about your sanity, whether you could keep it all together."

Chrysler's situation got worse, and its employees gave up even more to save the company. Through it all *Financial World* magazine called Iacocca ". . .the glue that held the Chrysler Corporation together when the company was about to fall apart."

Iacocca began to see double and have dizzy spells. Once when he was in Congress, he began to feel as if he was walking on eggs. He almost fainted and discovered he had a condition called vertigo. This is an inner ear problem that makes people dizzy and lose their balance.

The pressure and tension was beginning to get to Lee. At last his efforts were rewarded when Congress approved $1.5 billion in loan guarantees. The company could borrow this much money, and the government would guarantee to pay it back if Chrysler couldn't.

The banks proved harder to deal with than Congress had been. Chrysler owed money to 400 lending institutions that had opposed the loan guarantees passed by Congress. Finally, Chrysler executive Steve Miller persuaded all the bankers to sit down together and work out an agreement. The papers needed for the agreement made up nearly ten thousand documents. The printing bill alone was $2 million. If all the papers had been stacked on top of each other, they would have been seven stories tall.

Most of this mass of paper was stored in one of Chrysler's law firms in New York. A fire broke out in that building just hours before the papers were to be signed. Nervous bankers and Chrysler executives waited for fire fighters to control the blaze. In the middle of the night, executives carted critical papers out of the smoking building in mail carts. The next day, the loan agreements with the banks were completed.

The company also had to prove it was trying to save itself. Chrysler had to become slim and tough in order to use the money to its best advantage. Staying lean was always one of Iacocca's key points. Chrysler had to trim all unneeded workers and make every action count. It had no room for employees who did not perform their jobs well or for activities that did not contribute to profits.

The company's workers gave up $1.4 billion in benefits and wages. Many employees had to be retired, laid off, or fired. Iacocca reduced his pay to $1 a year, and management took average pay cuts of 5 percent. Lee learned that people will accept sacrifice when everyone is giving up something. Iacocca called it equality of sacrifice.

The company got support from many show business stars—Bob Hope, Bill Cosby, Pearl Bailey, and Frank Sinatra among others. Sinatra even made some commercials for $1 and stock options—the right to buy stock at a price which is lower than its current price on the stock market.

Lee worried about his employees' attitudes and the confidence of the public. The loan guarantees didn't mean anything if Chrysler workers couldn't build good cars and sell them.

A clerk named Lillian Zirwas at Chrysler's Lynch Road plant in Detroit wrote an article for the company paper about poor quality work. She told her fellow workers to take pride in their work and to improve company products. Iacocca asked her to come to his office so he could thank her for the article. Lillian decided to bake a cake for him. The cake was so good that Mary Iacocca asked her for the recipe, and then other people began asking for it. When Lillian made it for a wedding, a wedding guest offered to buy a Chrysler car if Lillian made her brother the same cake for his upcoming wedding. Lillian did, and the customer bought the car.

After Chrysler workers heard about the Lillian Zirwas cake story, no one dared to do careless work. Quality became obvious everywhere, and Iacocca needed it. Kenyon and Eckhardt, Chrysler's advertising agency, launched a campaign to raise employees' spirits and build public confidence. Bill Winn came up with the "We can do it!" slogan, followed by "Consider it done." Banners appeared everywhere. Then the company added the word "New" to its name to become the "New Chrysler Corporation."

Through all the problems, the one hope Iacocca had was the K-car. Hal Sperlich had been working on it since 1977. Iacocca believes it is the car they would have built at Ford if Henry Ford had let them. It would be an American made, fuel efficient, front wheel drive automobile—everything the American people said they wanted. Unfortunately, the plans for the K-car didn't go smoothly. Problems with the robot welders in the factory caused production snags. At first the car had too high a sticker price.

Iacocca's job was about to get even bigger. He became the person in Chrysler's ads and commercials trying to convince the public to buy the product. A survey taken by Kenyon and Eckhardt showed that 40 percent of the American people recognized Iacocca. He was a national figure, and Kenyon and Eckhardt believed that he could convince the public to buy Chrysler cars. Iacocca, however, was afraid it would seem as if the company was too desperate. He also didn't have the time. Finally, Lee agreed and he reviewed every script.

The commercials with Iacocca in them have been very successful. Some people believe his personality has helped sell more cars than anyone else could have. Lee doesn't believe that, however. "If the cars are good and the price is right, they'll sell." he says. The commercials have made him more well known than he already was, but they have also destroyed his privacy. Now strangers recognize him and often speak to him. Many tell him how much they admire him. Some praise their Chrysler cars, and others complain about them. Lee is amazed by the power television has to make people famous.

Slowly but surely, Chrysler began to recover. The 1981 report to company shareholders declared a loss of $475.8 million and called that an improvement over 1980 when the company lost $1.7 billion. Then the situation really took a turn for the better. In 1982 the company made a small profit! In the 1982 report to shareholders, Iacocca wrote, "We as a company are proud of our accomplishments, just as we are proud of our hard-working people, our products, and our role as a leader in the American automobile industry. With all that we have accomplished, we are now poised to take full advantage of better times in the year ahead."

By 1983 Chrysler was out of danger and making money. On July 13, 1983, Iacocca announced that Chrysler was paying back its loans early. And he did it five years to the day since Henry Ford II had fired him. "We at Chrysler borrow money the old-fashioned way. We pay it back," Lee said. Chrysler's executives held a ceremony in New York one month later. Iacocca gave the bankers a check for $813,487,500—the largest check he had ever seen.

Lee had these thoughts about his experience at Chrysler. "After forty years of hard work, I can say that responsibility brings mixed feelings—both pain and joy. At Chrysler we saved thousands of jobs, but we had to sacrifice others. That still hurts. You realize you can't accomplish everything you want."

Praise for Iacocca's leadership came even from within

the Ford Motor Company. A Ford executive once said, "There might be some other hotshot somewhere in the country who could have done as well, but I don't think anybody around the auto industry could have. Altogether, his particular savvy and guts and confidence in himself, plus the group he surrounded himself with, seemed to jell effectively."

The victory of repaying the government was not as sweet as it might have been. Mary was not at Lee's side to share the happiness of his greatest triumph. She had stood by Lee through all the years at Ford and Chrysler, celebrated his successes, and helped him live through the mistakes. Yet the diabetes she had suffered from all her life had taken its toll.

Mary had her first heart attack in 1978 after Lee was fired from Ford. In January 1980, she had a second attack, and in the spring of 1982, she suffered a stroke. Each of these major illnesses followed a period of major problems at Ford or Chrysler.

When Lee traveled, he called Mary several times a day. At night he made sure someone was home with her if he was away. Despite the care she received, on May 15, 1983, Mary Iacocca died before she could see Lee's triumph.

"Mary sustained me, and she gave everything she had to Kathi and Lia," says Lee. "Yes, I've had a wonderful and successful career. But next to my family, it really hasn't mattered at all."

Today, even though Chrysler is healthy and profit-ble, Lee Iacocca still spends most of his time away from home—at the office or on the road. No matter how busy his schedule, he always has and will continue to make time for his family. In a recent interview with *Redbook* magazine, he said, "There is probably some making up to do. Even during the tough time when they [his daughters] were growing up, I made a lot of time and spent a lot of time with them. I think I found a happy balance. I feel good. I hope they do. But I guess, to be honest, everybody says, 'I could have done more. I could have done more.'"

In 1986 Lee Iacocca added a new member to his family when he married Peggy Johnson, a former Pan American flight attendant. The marriage was a small ceremony and had its share of family problems. At first Lee's daughters did not approve of his decision to marry again, but they finally changed their minds about it. Unfortunately, this marriage did not last. Lee filed for a divorce nine months later.

(Top) *Lee Iacocca introduces two new Chrysler cars, including the minivan, at a press conference.* (Bottom) *Lee shows off the new K-car to reporters at a special ceremony.*

Lee Iacocca appears in one of his well-known Chrysler commercials.

At a ceremony to repay the last of Chrysler's U.S. government guaranteed loans, Lee Iacocca proposes a toast to celebrate the occasion.

(Top) *A billboard in Michigan advertises Lee Iacocca's autobiography.* (Bottom) *Lee with his mother, Antoinette Iacocca, to celebrate the publication of his autobiography.*

An automatic welding system at Chrysler Corporation's Windsor, Ontario, assembly plant uses computer-controlled robots to weld all new body openings on Chrysler wagons and vans.

Minivans roll off the final part of the assembly line at Chrysler's Windsor, Ontario, plant.

(Top) *At Chrysler's Sterling Heights, Michigan, assembly plant, robots use laser beams and electronic cameras to measure the body of the Chrysler Lebaron GTS/Dodge Lancer.* (Bottom) *Lee Iacocca introduces the new cars built at the Sterling Heights plant.*

Lee Iacocca puts on earmuffs to drown out the noise as a worker hammers on the base of the Statue of Liberty. Iacocca helped lead the effort to restore the Statue of Liberty and Ellis Island.

Chapter/Seven

Iacoccamania

Lee Iacocca is the kind of person people can't ignore. He seems to be either well liked or totally disliked. But whether or not you like him, you have to admire his ability to get things done—to set goals and stick to them no matter what.

For Iacocca the Chrysler victory was sweet. At the darkest times, the company declared losses of $1.7 billion. Chrysler executives juggled payments and delayed them as much as possible to keep the company afloat. Yet in 1983, Iacocca had pulled off one of modern business history's most amazing feats. He had taken the almost bankrupt company and not only rescued it, but turned it into a money-making organization. He says that he learned more in three years with Chrysler than in thirty-two years with Ford.

Many people in both business and government thought Lee Iacocca was all talk and no action. The *Wall*

Street Journal wrote that he was "Motor City's most famous motor mouth." But he has also been called one of the country's most skillful and successful managers. Chrysler's nearly 4,000 dealers love him. Many think he has helped boost Chrysler's auto sales. His commercials have reached more than 95 percent of American households, and people think he is one of the country's most honest men.

The word "Iacoccamania" has been created to explain how popular he is. Iacocca receives 4,000 requests to speak to groups each year. As a young man, Lee was nervous when he had to talk to groups. Today, he is such a good speaker that Bob Hope once complained when he had to perform after Iacocca. Hope swore he would never follow him onto the stage again.

Iacocca writes a newspaper column that appears in 350 papers. When his autobiography came out, it sold at the rate of 15,000 copies a day—more than the number of Chrysler cars sold per day. More than 1.5 million copies of the book were printed. Its success, though, will not make Lee Iacocca any richer. The book's profits are going to the Lee Iacocca Foundation and the Joslin Diabetes Center.

What is it about this tough-talking son of Italian immigrants that makes Americans rally behind him? Iacocca believes in the goodness of the United States and its people. He believes you can't do anything by yourself, and that you succeed by surrounding yourself with good people. Chrysler survived because so many groups of people worked together to make it happen. Of the 40,000 workers laid off, 25,000 have been called back to work.

"Now we've got some fantastic products, and the fun is to see how good you can make them," Lee says. He is putting the profits the company is making into space-age technology. But he was planning for the future even when the present was pretty grim.

When Chrysler was borrowing to stay open, Iacocca decided to develop the LeBaron convertible and minivan. Convertibles had been phased out in the late 1970s because of problems with safety standards. Still, Lee wanted a "fun" car, and he had a one-of-a-kind convertible made just for him. As he drove it one summer, other drivers pulled him over to ask him where he bought it and where they could buy it. Lee decided it was time to bring back the convertible. Once Chrysler decided to build it, orders for the car came from all over the country. The first one off the assembly line was delivered to Brooke Shields.

The minivan was another gamble Iacocca took back in the dark days when Chrysler was losing money. It took millions to convert the company's plant in Windsor, Ontario, to produce the minivan.

Once again, Iacocca had judged the public right. Chrysler had 100,000 more orders than it could fill when the new van came out. Iacocca believes that the minivan is a car that he and Hal Sperlich would have built for Ford if Henry Ford II had been willing to experiment with it.

Lee is committed to new technology. Computer controlled engines and electronic instrument clusters are built into many Chrysler cars. Robots and computers play important roles in Chrysler's commitment to quality and productivity. The company estimates that by 1988 it will use more than 1,000 robots to do more than 95 percent of its car manufacturing. In keeping with this commitment to use computer technology to its fullest, Chrysler has set up a Manufacturing Technical Center in Detroit.

"Right now, computer chips are not only helping us manufacture better quality cars more productively, but they're helping today's automobiles get better mileage, cleaner exhaust emissions, and better interior climate controls," says Lee. "After the military, American automakers are the high-technology industry's biggest customers."

The Sterling Heights Assembly Plant—the first new plant Chrysler built in twenty years—is one of the world's most advanced. New high-technology assembly lines take two days to assemble more than 3,700 parts into a car. More than 200 robots do body welding and heavy lifting. Laser cameras inspect more than 350 points of various parts of the car body as it moves down the six-mile assembly line. The whole operation is controlled by computers. The Dodge Lancer and Chrysler LeBaron GTS, built at the Sterling Heights Plant, are the first cars designed totally by computer.

"This is high-tech America, and more important, it's high-tech America at work," Iacocca says. "I've been telling people for years that you can't write off heavy industry and move only to high-tech in this country. You have to marry the two. You have to work together, and this is an example of what you get when you do."

Technology, however, is not the only key to success. Iacocca is a great believer in giving people the chance to create their own lives. He is comfortable in a barroom or a board room, and people sense that he is the kind of person who will be bluntly honest. In fact, Iacocca's tendency to say exactly what he thinks regardless of the results makes some people nervous. It is his outspokenness that may limit what he can do next.

Some people think he ought to run for president. A committee has been formed to draft Iacocca as a presidential candidate in 1988. Lee is honored by all the attention, but has stated that he is not a candidate and does not intend to become a candidate. However, he has also said in an article in *Life* magazine that if he wanted to be president, he could succeed.

Iacocca may not have the right personality to deal effectively with politicians. He is used to getting things done his own way and not spending days and weeks talking before he acts. Lee has thought about taking a job in the U.S. government that would give him some control over the economy. Washington, according to Iacocca, is borrowing and spending and leaving the bill for its children, tomorrow's adults. "So maybe we should hear from the kids on this subject. Maybe we should restrict the vote to those under thirty years old, because they're the ones getting stuck with the bills. . .My parents didn't live it up at my expense. They knocked themselves out to make sure I had more than they did. I think we owe the same thing to our country and our kids."

Iacocca thinks the "equality of sacrifice" that saved Chrysler can work for America to reduce the deficit—the money the country borrows to keep running. If everybody gave up something, says Iacocca, such as money from defense and social programs, and if everybody paid more taxes, the deficit would be reduced. In time all the money the government has borrowed could be repaid.

Lee Iacocca believes that our strengths as a country come from our roots—from the courage of the men, women, and children who arrived here from around the world. He served as chairperson of the nonprofit organization that raised money to save the Statue of Liberty and Ellis Island. This job, too, was touched by the colorful Iacocca personality. When his opinions clashed with the National Park Service, he was fired as head of an advisory commission on the Statue of Liberty and Ellis Island project. The firing resulted from a difference of opinion between Iacocca and the park service over how Ellis Island should be used. As usual, the public took sides in the Iacocca-centered conflict. Lee claims that the episode will be the subject of the first three chapters of his next book.

Despite this latest conflict, Iacocca is deeply committed to restoring the Statue of Liberty. He continued to serve as chairperson of the committee to raise money for the project. Lee says the Statue of Liberty stands for the beliefs of the immigrants who came here—the dignity of hard work and the fight for what is right.

Lee Iacocca believes that the future of America rests

in the hands of our young people. He has some advice for people growing up in today's world.

"If our grandparents could overcome, maybe you can too. You may never have thought about it, but they. . . gave up a lot. They wanted your life to be better than theirs. . .Apply yourself. Get all the education you can, but then. . .do something!"

Appendix

A Brief History
of the Automobile

1885 Gottlieb Daimler of Germany patented a high-speed four-stroke engine.

1893 Charles and J. Frank Duryea built the first successful internal combustion car in the United States.

1895 The Michelin brothers invented air-filled tires for automobiles.

  The first auto race was held in America on a course from Chicago to Waukegan, Illinois.

1896 The first traffic accident in the United States occurred in New York City. A Duryea Motor Wagon collided with a bicycle.

1898 Renault built the first totally enclosed car.

1902 The disc brake was patented.

1903 Henry Ford began the Ford Motor Company with twelve workers and a fifty-foot-wide plant.

1904 The Rolls Royce Corporation was founded by two Englishmen—Mr. Rolls and Mr. Royce.

The Stanley Steamer was built. It took thirty minutes to build up enough steam to start.

1906 Ford brought out the Model N, the first successful mass-produced car. It sold for $500.

The Michelins invented the first inflatable spare tire.

1908 Ford brought out the Tin Lizzie, the Model T.

William Crapo Durant merged several auto companies to form General Motors.

1911 The self-starter was perfected and was first used in the 1912 Cadillac.

1914 The first modern traffic light appeared in Cleveland, Ohio.

1924 Dodge produced the first all-steel automobile body for its cars.

1925 Walter Chrysler founded the Chrysler Corporation.

1937 Oldsmobile offered the first automatic transmission.

1938 The Volkswagen "beetle" was produced.

1939 Ford brought out the Mercury.

1951 Chrysler was the first to offer power steering.

1954 German engineers developed the rotary engine.

1956 Ford introduced the seat belt as an option in its cars.

1964 Ford introduced the Mustang.

1966 The National Traffic and Motor Vehicle Safety Act was passed. It created the National Traffic Safety Administration.

1970 The Clean Air Act was passed to require car exhaust to become purer.

1983 Chrysler introduced the new minivans— Plymouth Voyager and Dodge Caravan.

Bibliography

Abodaher, David. *Iacocca.* New York: Zebra Books, 1982.

Burlingame, Roger. *Henry Ford.* New York: Alfred A. Knopf, 1955.

Gambino, Richard. *Blood of My Blood: The Dilemma of the Italian Americans.* New York: Doubleday, 1974.

Gordon, Maynard M. *The Iacocca Management Technique.* New York: Ballantine, 1985.

Iacocca, Lee, with Novak, William. *Iacocca: An Autobiography.* New York: Bantam, 1984.

Lacey, Robert. *Ford: The Men and the Machine.* Boston: Little, Brown, 1986.

Lasky, Victor. *Never Complain. Never Explain. The Story of Henry Ford II.* New York: Richard Marek, 1981.

Moritz, Michael, and Seaman, Barrett, *Going for Broke: The Chrysler Story.* New York: Doubleday, 1981.

Index

DATE DUE		
MAR 2 2 1988		
FEB 4 1991		
MAR — 2 1993		
MAR 1 5 1994		
NOV 1 6 1998		
DEC 0 8 1998		
FEB 9 2001		

15095

92
IAC

Haddock, Patricia.

Standing up for
America : a
biography of Lee
Iacocca.